Pastels

Collins

30
minute

Pastels

Margaret Evans

First published in 2008 by
Collins, an imprint of
HarperCollins*Publishers*
77-85 Fulham Palace Road
Hammersmith, London W6 8JB

www.collins.co.uk

Collins is a registered trademark of HarperCollins Publishers Limited.

the author

oduced, stored
means,
ise, without

sh Library.

Designer: Kathryn Gammon

ISBN 978 0 00 726297 7

Colour reproduction by Colourscan, Singapore
Printed and bound by Printing Express, Hong Kong

Page 2: **Burano Houses,** 20 × 25 cm (8 × 10 in)

About the Author

Margaret Evans is a Past President of the Society for All Artists (SAA). She is best known for her pastel painting, but she also teaches watercolours, oils, acrylics and other media. She is internationally known for her portraits in oil and pastel, and is a member of the Portrait Society of America, the Pastel Society of America, Pastel Artists of Canada and L'Art du Pastel en France. She has exhibited her work with the Royal Society of Portrait Painters and the Pastel Society and features regularly in *International Artist* magazine. Margaret also runs successful workshops and painting holidays, and her numerous teaching videos and DVDs are available worldwide.
For more information, visit www.shinafoot.co.uk

Dedication
I dedicate this book to my long-suffering and lovely husband Malcolm, who always has faith in my achievements and helps me reach my goals, and to Robert Wade for giving me encouragement, inspiration and advice. Everyone needs a guru to aspire to!

Acknowledgements
My thanks to all my loyal students from far and near, who have stuck by me, travel great distances to be taught by me, and offer continuous support and friendship. My thanks also go to Caroline Churton at HarperCollins for choosing me as author and for all her encouragement, help and advice throughout, and to Diana Vowles, for her patience and skill in making my text understandable to all.

CONTENTS

INTRODUCTION

Using pastels is the most versatile and direct way to paint, as it is 'hands-on' and gives immediate results. Never has there been a better medium for adapting to 30-minute painting, especially when it comes to helping the amateur artist not only to gain confidence in achieving results quickly but also to gain confidence in painting outdoors, especially in changeable weather!

With pastels there is no need to set up water pots, brushes and palettes – it's as easy as using pencil on paper and a lot more fun. Their dry form makes them convenient to transport, but if you wish to you can add water and your pastels will turn into pure paint.

◀ **St Felix**
34 × 47 cm
(13½ × 18½ in)
Thirty minutes gave me just enough time to block in the golden fields and hazy blue distance on light brown paper.

Advantages of pastels

Pastels offer a variety of ways to paint. They can be soft and subtle, like the name suggests, or they can be strong and vibrant, which is often a surprise to the uninitiated. They come in all sorts of shapes and sizes, from fine pastel pencils to thick chunks of pure pigment, and offer the chance to use quick sketching techniques as well as fully fledged painting skills. Most commonly used as a dry medium, they can also be wetted to create imaginative textures and solid colour, and are very compatible with other media.

▶ **Highland Pathway**
23 × 23 cm (9 × 9 in)
Here I applied strong blocks of pastel colours thickly to a black paper to create dynamic contrasts and atmospheric tonal variations.

The 30-minute challenge

In 30 minutes you need to select the subject, plan the strategy, choose the angle and get it all down quickly! Outdoors you may be battling with unpredictable weather, and indoors snatching half an hour to do some quick painting may be tricky when there are many tasks you feel you should be doing. The best plan of attack is to be prepared and to keep everything simple.

Look at the subject and ask yourself what it is that attracts you and makes you want to paint it. This is the essence of your painting. Remembering this throughout your allotted time will help you to keep to the important point and not become distracted by inessentials.

The aim of this book

In this book, I have set out to encourage everyone to do something creative in 30 minutes. The essentials are to simplify the subject and not try to copy it exactly – look for the big shapes and the little shapes will follow. Remember that you are not attempting to reproduce a photographic reality but to communicate your vision of the subject to the viewer.

Anyone who has ever fancied being an artist but thinks they don't have the time will be amazed at what they can achieve in just half an hour. A complete and complicated work may not be possible but you will discover from *30-Minute Pastels* that satisfying and exciting paintings certainly are.

◀ **People at Caffe Rusilio**
11 x 25 cm (4½ x 10 in)
A quick sweep of colour around the umbrellas gives the setting for diners, leaving the mass shape of figures and umbrellas white.

ESSENTIAL EQUIPMENT

Good equipment will help you to get good results and will also make the job easier, but there is no point in setting yourself up with so much equipment that you don't know where to start. That takes up valuable time, and the less decision-making you have to do, the more time you have for concentrating on the job in hand – painting!

Always think carefully about what you really need. When you come home from a painting session outdoors, always put the things you actually used to one side and what you didn't use to the other – you will be shocked at what you have just hauled around for nothing, and you will be more selective next time.

◄ **Artists at Work**
25 × 30 cm (10 × 12 in)
Observing and sketching in the basic outlines of these artists took me only a few minutes and the rest of the time was spent building up the scene around them.

Pastels

Whether they are soft or hard, pastels are a dry medium. The only exception is oil pastel, which is oil-based and therefore feels greasier. It dilutes only with turps.

Soft, hard and pastel pencils are all compatible with each other and all have their own advantages to complement the others.

Soft pastels
The softer brands of pastel such as Sennelier and Daler-Rowney have a high percentage of pure pigment held together by binders and can feel crumbly or creamy in texture. They are ideal for solid colour applications in painting techniques and for filling in large areas quickly.

Hard pastels
Harder brands such as Conté Carres or NuPastel have less pigment, with fillers such as clay or kaolin added and binders to hold them together. They offer a finer point and are therefore ideal for sketching and drawing detail.

Pastel pencils
The pastel content inside these pencils tends to be of a harder consistency otherwise they would break too easily. They are ideal for sketching without being messy, easy to carry and excellent for detail work. They are best sharpened with a craft knife to expose the pastel core, then used on their side to work into a point.

QUICK TIP

Choose a pastel type that suits you – some people prefer soft, crumbly ones, but pencils and hard sticks are neater and tidier to use.

◄ **Pastel types**
Pastels range from the soft, creamy varieties to harder, thinner sticks and pastel pencils.

◄ Soft pastels
Soft pastels need very little pressure to produce a solid block of colour but are more difficult to control for thinner marks and are more likely to smudge.

▲ Hard pastels
Hard pastels keep their shape, can still block colour solidly, but also offer thinner line work for finer detail and quick sketching.

◄ Pastel pencils
Pastel pencils are ideal for sketching and detail work, as well as blocking in small areas of colour.

◀ **Market Day, Mirepoix**
25 × 30 cm (10 × 12 in)
This example of pastel on a dark blue paper shows the strong effects created by using bright colours thickly to cover the dark base and create light areas and thinly where darker, shadowy tones are needed, allowing the paper to show through.

Surfaces

There are many types of ideal surfaces for pastel, including papers and boards, but all must offer a reasonable 'tooth' in order for the pastel to grip well, which helps to avoid smudging. From slight weaves to abrasive sandpapers, the surface plays an important role in pastel painting and has to suit the quantity of pastel being applied – a thick application of soft pastels needs an abrasive surface to grip the medium well, whereas a lighter weave paper is sufficient for sketching with hard pastels or pencils.

▶ **Pastel papers**
One of the most exciting elements of pastel painting is the wide variety of paper colours and textures that is available.

Other equipment

It would be easy to load yourself down with all the best equipment, including an easel, stool, parasol and table as well as the full range of top-quality pastels, but that would take about 30 minutes to set up! I have a telescopic easel that leaps into position quickly, with a shelf to hold my tray of chosen pastels, hard and soft, and a board with a folder attached which also holds my papers and finished works in place. I leave the rest of my gear at the studio for longer painting sessions.

▶ **Equipment**
Other items you might find useful include fixative, a paper torchon and masking tape for holding down your paper. To wet the pastels for painterly effects you will also need brushes and a palette.

MAKING MARKS

Pastel is tactile and direct, and therefore time-saving. Every mark made means something, whether it is a thin line or a strong block of colour, which makes it an ideal medium for 30-minute sketching and painting.

Learning the difference between linear and painterly marks along with blocking, layering and glazing techniques will teach you how to control the amount of pastel you place in each area of the painting. It will also help you to discover how to cover the paper colour or allow it to show through, depending on the pressure of the mark you choose to make.

◀ **Loch and Trees**
30 × 48 cm (12 × 19 in)
Sometimes drawing is not necessary; simple bold blocks of colour, varying the direction of the strokes as I have done here, can create a quick impression of a scene.

Linear marks

By using the end of the pastel stick you can make single lines for drawing outline shapes or repeated side strokes to build up a body of colour, either parallel to each other or cross-hatched to give colour mixing and texture.

Lines

To create a single drawing line for outlining and positioning the subject on the page, hold the stick like a pencil and use the end. Vary the pressure to create thin or thick lines and you will discover how crumbly or hard your pastel brand is. You can sharpen hard pastels if you want a pointed edge and pastel pencils are ideal for this; use them slightly on their side to avoid continually blunting the point as you work.

◄ **Linear marks**
Varying the pressure will give you thicker or thinner marks.

▶ **Outlines of Florence**
Using pencils or hard pastels, you can draw simple outline shapes to set out composition ideas then fill them in later with blocks of colour.

Side strokes

By holding the stick at a lower angle to the paper and repeating the mark more closely, you can build up a mass of colour which fills in areas quickly. The pressure that you use will determine a strong block of colour or a light shade which still allows the paper colour to show through.

Cross-hatching

Using the stick as for side strokes, make marks by building up strokes in opposite directions, either using the same colour to create density or varying them to colour mix. To make further colour mixes add more layers on top, each layer in a different direction from the last.

◀ **Highland Loch**
17 × 28 cm (6½ × 11 in)
After sketching in the scene I quickly placed the colours and shapes with side strokes and cross-hatching, building up directional strokes to give atmosphere.

◀ **Pathway**
25 × 20 cm (10 × 8 in)
Using pencils or hard pastel sticks, colour can be built up by cross-hatching. This creates a solid mass of colour and helps the eye to 'mix' colours applied on top of each other.

▲ **Side strokes**
Holding the pastel at an angle, repeat lines to build colour.

▲ **Cross-hatching**
Making opposite side strokes allows you to mix colours.

Painterly marks

By breaking a pastel stick in half and holding the stick on its side, you can produce a block of colour in a similar way to using a flat brush in painting. These painterly marks are ideal for blocking in larger areas of a painting, and speed up the process of covering paper as well as building up strong colour patterns.

Blocking
Holding the stick on its side, put the full width of the pastel on the paper to create a solid mark of colour for filling in or showing strong colour.

Glazing
Holding the pastel lightly on its side, drag it over previous layers. This shows the colour underneath and you can build layers up into glazes, similar to washes in oils or watercolours.

▶ **Blocking**
Blocking in colour with the side of the pastel stick is the quickest way to cover a large area and capture the essence of the scene.

▶ **Glazing**
Glazing gives exciting colour mixes when one colour is layered on top of another and is a useful technique for creating misty, atmospheric effects.

▲ **Sunflowers**
19 × 25 cm (7½ × 10 in)
Blocks of colours create an immediate impression of this scene. Glazing colours over each other in the fields gives a feel of the varying hues that occur as the crops move in the breeze.

▶ Stippling
Broken dots of
pigment allow
the paper
colour to
intersperse with
the pastel colours
and give a different
colour visually.
Adding further
colours allows the
eye to mix them
visually.

▶ Broken colour
Broken colour is
useful on textured
papers to create
further textured
areas. Varying the
size of the strokes
will create movement
and interest.

Stippling
Stippling pigment on with the end of
the stick builds up a dotted effect, giving
a vibrant and exciting appearance to the
picture; you can place different colours
side by side to create strong, colourful
textures. You can also achieve a sense
of recession by varying the size of the
dots, reducing them as they go into
the background.

Broken colour
Broken strokes or blocks of colour can
be used for vibrant shimmering effects,
creating a texture and liveliness which
can sometimes be lost in pastels when
an area is blended. Broken colour is a
particularly successful technique on
rough papers, where the pattern of the
paper texture adds to the vibrancy of
the effect.

▶ Tuscan Doorway
24 × 19 cm (9½ × 7½ in)
For old buildings
with textured and
crumbling walls,
stippling and broken
colour are ideal for
creating a busy area.
They work especially
well against smooth
blended areas to
create a contrast of
textures, adding
interest to a painting.

◀ **Layering**
By layering colours on top of each other you can create mixes and new colours. The same colour layered on top of itself will create a stronger, more solid version, covering the paper texture.

▼ **Stone Wall**
14 × 20 cm (5½ × 8 in)
The bottom layers of colour become smoother as the top layers push the pastel into the paper, and texture is created on top to capture the many facets of stones and boulders. This technique is ideal for foregrounds.

QUICK TIP

Remember that layering is basically colour mixing that takes place on the paper rather than on a palette, giving a dynamic and expressive result.

Layering

Layering is best used for mixing colours, as one colour on top of another can blend to give subtle and varying results, especially on brickwork, stonework and so forth; you can layer colour on colour until you achieve what you are looking for. This process of building up layers of pastel creates a thick and thin balance throughout the painting. Where you want the paper colour and texture to be part of the finished appearance, apply the layers of pastel lightly; if you want a smoother finish, apply solid layers of colour.

Blending

Blending is a method of rubbing in the pastel to create smoother effects – but it is one of the most overused and abused techniques, as it can lead to dull, overworked paintings. In a 30-minute pastel, keep blending to a minimum.

You can achieve a fresh, painterly approach by applying the pastel with other techniques, then finishing with a light touch of blending to smooth out a few areas such as skies to give the picture a rough and smooth balance. Blending is mostly done by rubbing with fingers, but you can also use tissue, paper torchons or rubber blenders.

▲ **Scottish Sky**
15 × 23 cm (6 × 9 cm)
Blending for basic sky colours is effective to smooth the area before adding clouds. This is also particularly useful to contrast a smooth sky with a textured subject.

◀ **Blending**
Where two or more colours are mixed on top of each other you can blend them to create a solid colour, covering the paper and giving softer edges.

QUICK TIP

Blending is often better done back at the studio after some thought rather than spending valuable time on it outdoors and perhaps overusing it.

Adding water

Adding water to pastel gives it a whole new look, as the dry pigment turns into paint. You can also dilute pastel with turpentine to create the effect of a thin oil painting. This painterly appearance gives more strength to the argument that pastel is a serious painting medium as well as a sketching tool.

There are three ways of using water with pastel. Applying a damp brush with excess water sponged out to pastel gives solid colour as strong as oil or acrylic. Using a wet brush has the opposite effect, diluting the colour and creating wash effects similar to watercolour. You can also apply the pastel to dampened paper, which enriches the colour.

◀ **Cream Roses**
22 × 27 cm (8½ × 10½ in)
For a watercolour finish the technique of adding water to pastel is ideal. Here I used it for creating soft glazes of colour, then for intensifying the colours on the roses and solidifying the foliage shapes.

▶ **Damp brush**
Wetting the pastel with a damp brush intensifies the colour and makes it appear more solid. This is ideal for areas where the paper colour needs to be covered.

▶ **Wet brush**
Wetting the area of pastel with a brush loaded with plenty of water dilutes the pigment. This makes it a useful way of spreading the colour over larger areas and also for laying in base colours for dry pastel to be added on top.

▶ **Damp paper**
Another way to intensify the richness of pastel colour is to apply dry pastel to a dampened area of paper. This is ideal for flower painting, where intense colour is needed without any background colour showing through.

◄ **Trossachs Barn**
30 × 23 cm (12 × 9 in)
I blocked in the colours on white paper, then wetted the pastel to spread the colour and cover the white. It created a fluid, watercolour appearance and helped to fix the pastel, effectively turning it into pure paint.

QUICK OVERVIEW

☐ Linear marks are used for drawing outline shapes and building up colour.

☐ Painterly marks are used for blocking in larger areas.

☐ You can mix colours in pastels by putting layers of different colours on top of each other.

☐ Blending creates smoother effects.

☐ Pastel is constituted of pure pigment and as such can be wetted with either water or turpentine to turn it into paint.

Exploring different textures

For this first project, experiment with creating textures. Try different varieties of pastels on a range of surfaces and see how diluting the pigments gives you further options to explore.

Dry applications for texture
Using different types of pastel, make dry applications on various paper textures. Rough papers will give a broken effect, leaving the paper colour showing through, while smoother papers with less tooth will give a more solid colour.

Wet techniques for diluted colour
Experiment with different types of pastel to see which ones dissolve better when water is added. To dilute the colour, use a wet brush; this will also be ideal for washes of smooth colour, rather like watercolour washes. Some pastels will melt easily into the water and others will resist, creating a different effect again.

◀ **Diluted colour**
Adding water with a wet brush dilutes the colour so that it spreads into a wash, making it suitable for smooth areas.

▶ **Dry pastel**
Dry pastel applied to white paper will always show up the texture of the surface unless it is blended to smooth it down.

Damp techniques for solid colour
Applying a damp brush rather than a wet one to pastel will give glorious rich, vibrant colour that will solidify to a smooth block, covering any paper colour and texture underneath. When you try

▲ **Solid colour**
Applying a damp brush over dry pastel creates solid colour ideal for strong subjects and pure colour for flowers.

this, notice how different the result is from using a wet brush, widening your range of possibilities.

Right technique, right subject
Select a few subjects and decide which techniques will most suit each area within them. Dry blocking in and a little blending is ideal for cloudy skies, whereas diluted pastel is good for washing in large areas of landscape. Dry pastel on top of wet washes is also useful for creating texture.

▲ **Hudson River, USA**
20 × 33 cm (8 × 13 in)
I put down random colours to suggest a landscape then added water with a large flat brush to create a base. I applied dry pastel on top in order to pull the composition together and add some texture.

▲ **Old Doorway**
25 × 20 cm (10 × 8 in)
I applied light neutral grey pastel to cream paper then washed over it. While it was still damp, I dragged new colours over the walls to give an old 'distressed' effect. Once the previous colours had dried out I built up dry pastel on top.

TONAL VALUES

Capturing the tonal values – the contrasts of light and dark – is the backbone of painting; without them, a painting is flat. The artist starts with a two-dimensional sheet of paper and has to try to create the third dimension, which is done by using tone to show form. By establishing tone quickly the 30-minute pastel will fall into place, even if the accuracy of colour comes later, through memory, photographic back-up or pure imagination.

Squinting at the subject with half-closed eyes will help you to block out the less important half-tones and the stronger contrasts of light and dark will emerge without detail to distract you.

◀ **Glenelg, Scotland**
23 × 30 cm (9 × 12 in)
Subtle tonal variations create an atmospheric mood, with a limited use of colours giving a low-key effect.

10-minute tonal studies

On white paper, you can work with simplified tonal values using just three tones – light, medium and dark. The light is the white paper, grey is mid-tone and black is dark. Imagine this as being on a scale of 1–100 per cent, from white to black.

When you are choosing a coloured paper on which to work with pastel, it is important to assess straight away if the paper is light, medium or dark in tone. If it is a mid-tone, you can use white for highlights and black for darks; if the paper is a dark tone such as black, mid-tones and highlights can be added with grey and white.

Colour and tone

You do not have to use black for dark tones and white for light. Even if the paper is a mid-tone value, you can identify the three tones with cream and brown pencils, using the paper colour as the mid-tone.

When you are selecting your colour range for paintings with more than the three basic tones, consider the tonal values of each colour you plan to use and make sure they cover the range from light to dark.

▲ The three main tones: white, grey and black, which represent light, medium and dark.

▌QUICK TIP

Shading in with a black pastel as lightly as possible then applying more pressure until you achieve pure black is a good way of learning about tonal values.

◀ **Hen**
Using one colour but varying the tone by increasing or decreasing the pressure with which you apply the pastel will give your subject excellent variety of light and shade.

▲ Italian House
17 × 14 cm (6½ × 5½ in)
With just four pastel
pencils selected to
cover four tonal
variations, a quick
sketch of a house
gave me enough
information to do an
entire painting later.

▲ Mexican Sunset
20 × 30 cm (8 × 12 in)
A dark grey paper
offered me the
perfect contrast on
which to paint a

vibrant Mexican
sunset quickly, using
just five colours
which span the tonal
range of light,
medium and dark.

Working in monochrome

The best way to explore as many tonal variations as possible is to try a study using one colour only, ideally of a dark tone such as dark green. By varying the pressure on the paper, it is possible to achieve even five or six varying shades of that colour, including the paper tone.

A more challenging study is to see how many tones you can achieve with a colour range such as yellow or red. These are often thought to be 'light' colours, but by putting them against each other you will find their tonal values easier to evaluate.

▶ **Indian Canoe**
23 × 25 cm (9 × 10 in)
Varying the pressure when applying one colour can give plenty of different tonal values, making quick sketching even simpler with less to carry and less to think about!

▼ **Dancer**
26 × 22 cm (10 × 8½ in)
Without including
details of her
features, the pose
of this dancer could
be quickly captured
to create the mood
in shades of red.

▲ **Yellow Sky**
20 × 30 cm (8 × 12 in)
Yellow is thought of
as a light tone but
with different types of
yellow against a dark
background, variations
can give drama and
keep the palette to
a minimum.

Using a limited tonal range

You have learnt to think of black and white as a scale of 1–100 per cent; now, to create mood and subtlety, try to restrict this range of tones to 30–70 per cent. This means creating a softer range, not using anything as dark as black or as light as white. This makes for a more challenging perception of tonal ranges but is ideal for changing the mood of a subject, not only in misty landscapes for atmospheric effect but also for subtlety in portraiture, for example.

▲ **Eilean Donan Mists**
20 × 28 cm (8 × 11 in)
I kept the range of tones close together in this painting to give a soft, moody atmosphere that suited the subject.

▼ Villefranche-sur-Mer
33 × 46 cm (13 × 18 in)
I quickly captured the strong sunlight on these colourful buildings by contrasting the tonal values on a wide scale.

Using a wider tonal range

By extending that range of colours to cover a wider tonal scale, the drama and clarity of a scene can be changed, particularly in strong sunshine. Many paintings lack a sense of strong sunlight, simply because the tonal range is not wide enough. The more contrast, the stronger the sunshine will appear.

QUICK OVERVIEW

☐ At its simplest, your tonal range can consist of just three tones: light, medium and dark.

☐ Working in monochrome makes quick sketching even simpler.

☐ The tonal range of a picture can be narrow to create moody, atmospheric, low-key paintings or wide to achieve impact and drama.

Sketching tonal values

In even the simplest sketch, exploring the tonal values of your subject will bring it to life. On location it is important to sketch in your **tonal contrasts first** as the light will change constantly, affecting them while you work.

MATERIALS USED

Canson white
   sketching paper
Carb Othello dark
   grey pastel pencil
Soft pastels
Burnt sienna
Cream
Deep ochre
French
   ultramarine
Orange
Pale blue
Pinky-grey
Raw umber
Reddish brown
Sea green

1 With the dark grey pastel pencil, outline the shapes of each chicken, making sure they interact as shown here. Once you have established the basic composition, use the pastel pencil to block in shadows in order to create a strong tonal image and record the direction the light is coming from.

2 Add your colours lightly enough to allow the shadows to show through. Put in a few soft background colours to anchor the chickens to the ground and show the reflection of the foreground chicken in the puddle.

3 Strengthen the colours to create impact, especially on the large chicken, whose rich red-brown colours help to make the softer-coloured chicken come forward. The background chicken is basically gold; use hints of this colour in the large chicken to link the two, and blend the colours you used in the ground into the feathers of each bird. Strengthen the soft colours in the foreground to make the puddle stand out and darken the reflection.

SIMPLIFYING COLOURS

When you are working quickly, it is important to see colours in a simplified manner. Rather than looking for an exact match in your pastel collection it is fastest to record the basic colour and then add a few additional colours on top to show what adjustments are needed. Using thick or thin applications of pastel will allow the paper colour to play a part in the picture where it is of most use, which also helps to save time and give impact.

It is better to overstate than understate in painting and use your imagination – relying on the camera to record the subject often leads to disappointing and understated paintings.

◀ **Californian Landscape**
20 × 35 cm (8 × 14 in)
A painting should have 'impact colours' that immediately portray the mood and colours of the landscape. Here the hot red paper blends with the strong golds and yellows to create an impression of a hot country.

A limited palette

Colours fall into three categories: the three primary colours red, blue and yellow, which cannot be made by mixing other colours together; secondary colours, made by mixing two primary colours together, such as orange and purple; and tertiary colours, which are neutral colours such as browns and greys containing all three primary colours, or a primary and secondary colour.

A valuable method of working quickly is to simplify your choices of colour; a limited palette saves time and encourages you to put down colour information simply and boldly. A minimum palette could contain approximately 10 pastels – one each of yellow, red, blue, orange, purple and green, three neutrals and white. You can subsequently add your favourite colours to make the choice more personal, helping to develop an individual colour scheme or style that will become recognizable as your work.

▶ **Choosing colours**
Using a basic palette will ensure that colour mixing can be achieved just as in any other medium. After this, the fun is in supplementing the pastel box with extras.

Lemon Yellow   Cadmium Red   French Ultramarine

Orange   Purple   Green

| Naples Yellow | Raw Sienna | Burnt Umber | Burnt Sienna | Sky Blue | Blue Grey | Indigo | Dark Green |

◀ **Indian Girls**
Thin Conté sticks are useful for sketching brightly coloured figures for street scenes, such as these Indian girls in their saris.

Colour themes

You can use colour themes to enhance a scene by limiting yourself to different tones and tints of one main colour – for example, a painting done in variations of green. This method of working creates a mood and helps to emphasize tonal qualities. It also saves time when you are making a painting in 30 minutes, particularly if you decide on the colour theme in advance.

◄ **French Landscape**
23 × 33 cm (9 × 13 in)
This painting is predominantly a green scene with yellow golds. The contrast of the dark aubergine paper offers a relief from the greens and creates a background for shadow areas.

The colour wheel

Keeping a mental image of the most basic of colour wheels will help you to decide quickly on colour. By visualizing the wheel in three segments of the primary colours red, blue and yellow, you can quickly work out which colours will complement each one as these will be a mix of the other two colours.

For example, if the scene is predominantly reds, varying from rusty brown reds to purplish-reds, a green (a mix of blue and yellow) will be complementary to all of them. Although more complex colour wheels are useful, this approach keeps choosing colours simple and saves time.

◄ **Three-colour wheel**
This simplest of colour wheels can be easily imagined or roughly sketched on to the corner of a painting to act as a reminder of the complementaries.

▼ **Complementary colours**

yellow/purple

green/red

blue/orange

▲ **Hudson River Farm, USA**
23 × 33 cm (9 × 13 in)
The strong light was best captured by using black paper to help create strong shadows and accentuate the red/green balances of the composition.

Complementary balances

Working with pastels, you also have the option of choosing a paper in a complementary colour to the main theme of your painting, or in a colour that will emphasize the complementary colours you are applying. As opposite colours create a strong balance, using them will give you an instant impact for 30-minute works. As soon as the opposite colour is added to a coloured paper, it seems to vibrate and create an exciting reaction.

▶ **Indian River Scene**
25 × 20 cm (10 × 8 in)
The red paper provided the strong red balance against a very green scene, breaking up these greens to create more movement and vibrancy.

◀ **Spanish Rock House**
23 × 28 cm (9 × 11 in)
Hot orange and stark white are the predominant colours in this study, with blue paper providing a complementary balance.

Colour temperature

Certain colours are recognized generally as being either warm or cool – for example, red is thought of as a warm colour and blue is cool.

However, it is important to realize that within each category there are warmer and cooler versions. For example, French Ultramarine, which is more purple-orientated, is a warm blue, while Phthalo Blue and Prussian Blue are cooler; reds tending towards purple have blue in them, and are therefore cooler than reds tending towards orange, which are warmer.

Coloured papers

Hot scenes look great on a cool-coloured paper, and cool scenes such as snowy landscapes are stunning on hot red or orange papers. Once you have found success in balancing these together, it is exciting to try painting hot on hot and cold on cold instead, applying the opposites to shadows in order to create the same balance.

When you are using neutral papers, including white, you will need to build up the painting with balances of warm and cool colours. However, a great time-saver for the 30-minute pastel is to use opposite-coloured papers to begin with as they help to create instant impact.

▲ **Lucca, Tuscany**
23 × 30 cm (9 × 12 in)
Here the warm ochres and yellows of the buildings are exaggerated by the hot red paper, so I used strong blues to cool down the shadow areas and create a warm/cool balance.

QUICK TIP

Learn to assess the subject quickly as a generally warm or cool one – there will be both warm and cool in all subjects, but a first impression will tell you which to create as the dominant tone in your painting.

▲ **Cuillins from Sligachan, Skye**
25 × 38 cm (10 × 15 in)
A cold blustery day on Skye in Scotland would look really chilly on blue paper, but painting on to hot terracotta colour gives an underlying warmth and added drama that suits the mountains known as the Red Cuillins.

◄ **Cuillins from Carbost, Skye**
17 × 28 cm (6½ × 11 in)
I created a different mood by using white paper to depict a similar view of the Cuillins, adding warm and cool balances with pastel instead of relying on the paper colour for this.

Combining colour and tone

When you are combining colour and tone, it is important to have a clear idea of the sensation you want to create with your painting. Impact is important to attract the viewer's attention, but not all subjects are suitable for a dramatic approach – something more subtle and atmospheric may be the answer. The combination of tonal variation and a good balance of colour is the secret to success in both low-key and high-key themes.

▲ **Yellow and Blue Boats, Venice**
23 × 30 cm (9 × 12 in)
The strong Italian sunshine catching the primary colours of the boats in Chioggia, Venice, makes them stand out against the lightly painted background buildings, which melt slightly into the dark brown paper.

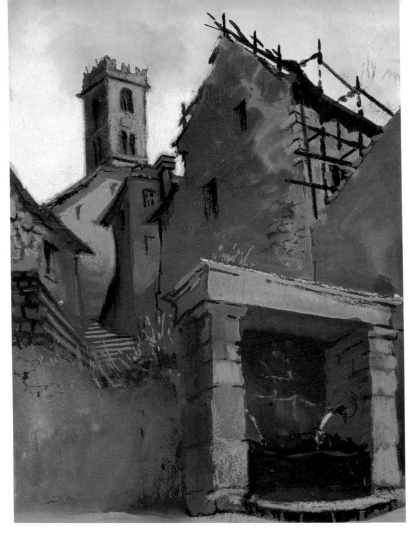

◀ **Tuscan Village**
30 × 23 cm (12 × 9 in)
The day was dark and thundery, and low in tonal variation. Using a terracotta paper for underlying warmth, I added washes of grey-blue over the building areas then gave them more detail with thin, light touches of colour. I put in the sky as a stronger contrast against the buildings.

QUICK OVERVIEW

☐ To simplify colours, limit your choices to save time on decision-making and mixing.

☐ Use complementary colours to give balance and impact.

☐ Make sure you include a balance of warm and cool colours.

☐ Take advantage of coloured papers to give you complementary and warm or cool colours.

◀ **Warm and cool**
Place a green and a purple and a purplish pink and an orange either side of your blues and reds respectively to identify which are warm or cool.

▼ **Emphasizing shapes**
Setting cool colours against warm and light tones against dark makes shapes stand out.

Exploring colour and tone

For a 30-minute painting, it is important to save time by limiting your colours. However, make sure that each colour works for its keep, not only on its own merits but also in terms of the effect it will have upon the other colours you have chosen.

Colour temperature

Take some blues or reds, and lay them in order from cool to warm. For example, since you add blue to red to make purple, a red that goes towards a purplish-pink tint will be cooler than a red that goes towards orange, made by adding yellow. In a blue range, the blue that goes towards purple will be warmer than the blue that cools off into green.

This exercise will make you more aware of different effects you can achieve by placing two colours together, and this will help you to save time when you are choosing your palette.

Tonal relationships

Draw a simple hill shape then put a pale sky blue above it and warm greens on the hill. Try different greens next to the sky blue to see how many different moods can be achieved. Next, draw the same shape, put a strong warm blue sky behind it and use cooler, lighter greens on the hill. The hill now stands out as a lighter shape against the darker tone, in contrast to the first one.

Draw the same simple hill shape with a blue-grey pastel and fill it in. Next, draw the outline of the hill but fill in the sky instead, leaving the hill as white paper. You can see from trying out these exercises that every colour also has a tonal depth which can be used to make shapes stand out.

cool against warm

light against dark

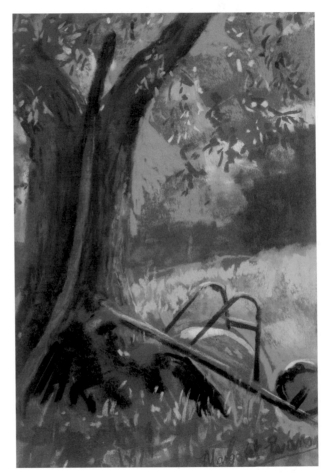

◀ Warm paper
Against this bright red paper, the blue of the hill is very cool.

◀ Cool paper
On cool blue paper, adding a touch of pink to the sky provides some contrasting warmth.

Coloured paper

All judgement of colours and tones is dependent upon what they are seen next to, so changing the paper colour will also change the tone and colour relationship of each pigment you work with. Try the same simple exercise on a red paper, then on a blue paper to see how the concept of warm and cool colours changes. If you find this confusing, remember to keep it simple and be aware of the choice of paper colour right at the start of your painting. If it is a hot scene, try a cool blue paper; for a cold scene, choose a warm one.

▶ Tuscan Wheelbarrow
25 × 18 cm (10 × 7 in).
The bright sunlight against the dark tree trunk inspired me to use a dark blue paper and highlight strong contrasts for impact.

PICTURE BUILDING

It is all too easy to become involved in detailed drawing and run out of time to paint! For a 30-minute painting you'll find that a plan for time allocation is essential, together with a mental summary of how you are going to tackle the most vital points, such as composition and light source.

Remember that your intention should be to capture an artist's impression of the subject rather than making a photographic replica. When you have only 30 minutes to spend on the painting, you need to concentrate on what is important and not make any attempt to copy everything slavishly.

◄ **French Fields in June**
33 × 47 cm (13 × 18½ in)
The crop fields and sunflowers create a wonderful pattern of textures leading up to the hilltop village in the distance.

Sketching in

The sketching-in stage is a method which, with practice, you will be able to do in five minutes, allowing maximum time for painting. It's a matter of learning to see the big shapes instead of all the details, and allowing your line to simplify these shapes and join areas together, rather like taking a line for a walk.

Line

Focus on the big shapes only and divide the page into main areas, for example land, sky and foreground. If the subject involves many shapes such as houses or trees, see them as one large shape rather than individual items, which will allow the drawing to take shape in minutes.

Composition

While you are making the line drawing, be aware of how shapes link up together and balance. Avoid placing your focal points too centrally and drawing shapes that take your eye out of the picture. Imagine that your picture is divided into thirds horizontally and vertically and place your points of interest a third of the way in from any edge (known as the rule of thirds). Ideally, a good composition should allow the viewer's eye to meander through the painting, not be led out of the frame or straight to the centre.

◀ **Linear sketch**
A rough outline has been sketched in to work out the positions of the main shapes. The skyline of trees and bushes is one large shape.

▶ **Composition sketch**
The pillar added on the right leads the eye from the back of the path across the left side and down the opposite pillar.

◀ **Exploring the format**
It is always worth while spending a few minutes playing about with different formats to see if the proportion of the main features is improved.

Proportion

Sketching in the large shapes first helps you to avoid making smaller shapes such as buildings, people and trees too big and discovering that you have run out of space on your paper. The larger shapes will contain the smaller ones, and by accommodating them comfortably in the painting will make it easier for you to place the small details later.

◀ **Sketching-in stage**
The basic linear shapes are drawn in with a colour that will feature in the painting – in this case, a dark green. The paper is mid-tone warm ochre, which will play a part in the earthy colour scheme underlying the greenery.

Blocking in

The blocking-in stage lays the main building blocks of colour on to the painting quickly, and should take no more than 10 minutes, which allows 15 minutes for the final stages and details. You can capture sudden changes of light source at this stage, and putting in shadows early will keep the essence of the picture fresh.

Pastel blocks

Breaking pastel sticks to a workable size, such as half or a third in length, makes it easy for you to apply them by holding the side of the stick and blocking in colour. Laying the pastel on with varying pressure will give you thick or thin marks which can be used to cover the paper colour or let it show through respectively, which in turn affects the colour and tone.

Pastel layers

The next step is to layer pastel on top of your previous layers, adjusting tonal shading, intensifying colour, mixing new colours directly on the paper and building up body on the painting. Some papers will take only a limited amount of layers before the pastel slips and is more difficult to apply, but better papers with abrasive surfaces will grip the pastel and hold many more layers.

◀ **Pastel blocks**
Blocking in with the side of a broken pastel stick is like painting with a flat brush, and gives a painterly stroke which helps to cover the area quickly.

▶ **Pastel layers**
After the initial blocking in of basic colours, further layers can be added to adjust the colour and tone of the mix to suit the subject.

◀ **Blocking-in stage**
Exaggerating the
light and dark tones
initially captures
changing light and
gives impact to
the subject at this
early stage.

Colour and tone

Colours at this stage will be approximate.
It is more important to overstate rather
than understate, so apply strong colours –
for example, a pinky-grey wall can be
quickly blocked in pink and made more
subtle and grey in later stages. Stressing
the tones early helps to allow for the
changes of light that are inevitable
outdoors and even occur with indoor
subjects. Keep the colour range limited to
avoid the composition becoming bitty.

Building up

The building-up stage is fun, as you have 15 minutes left! Working around the painting in a circular method, build up each section with detail at the focal points and layers of extra colours elsewhere. This stage is all about 'pushing and pulling'. Some features of the composition may need to be given more importance and can be pulled forward by detailing or sharpening the tonal values, whereas other areas that are too prominent will need pushing back with glazes of overlaying colours to quieten them.

Blending

At this stage, some areas will need blending to create a smoother finish, either because the paper is textured and rough, or to soften colours that have been mixed together. You can do this with your fingers, but it is important not to carry too much colour from one area to another otherwise everything becomes muddy and flat. Blending can also be done by pulling a harder pastel over soft pastels. This makes less of a colour change, and pushes the previous pastel into the paper surface more, creating the smoother effect.

Textural marks

Apart from the texture you will obtain simply by applying pastel to abrasive papers, you can make textural marks by stippling, cross-hatching and applying broken colour, all of which can create depth. Colours laid on top of each other, with parts of each colour still showing, will add volume and interest to your painting. You can also add texture with final detailed marks made with pencils or a fine dampened brush.

Interesting pictures contain variety, so don't be afraid to leave some areas understated and lacking texture.

▶ **Blending**
After blocking and layering there will be some areas of colour that need blending, perhaps to give a smoother finish or simply to banish the underlying colour of the paper.

◀ **Textural marks**
Additional mark-making such as stippling and broken colour, especially in areas such as gardens, can add further depth to the painting.

▲ Guiraude Lavender
32 × 47 cm
(12½ × 18½ in)
Finally detail is built
up in some areas and
others are left as
suggestions. It is
important not to
overwork or fiddle
with a picture or its
freshness will be lost.

Quick studies

Limiting your time on a painting is an excellent way of making sure you take down the important details first and guarantees there is no time for fussing over it or fiddling with too much detail. A fresh, sketchy approach is always better than a tired, overworked painting.

Practise this by seeing how much you can get down in 10-minute studies, then limit yourself even further to five minutes. By disciplining yourself to work in this small timescale you will find that your work will automatically become fresher, your speed will pick up, and outdoor painting will not seem so scary. Remember that putting the big shapes in first makes the whole picture appear more quickly; the smaller ones can follow in the time remaining.

▶ **French Windmill**
30 × 23 cm (12 × 9 in)
It was important to fit the large shape of the windmill and sails into the page to capture the overall shape of the subject in the composition.

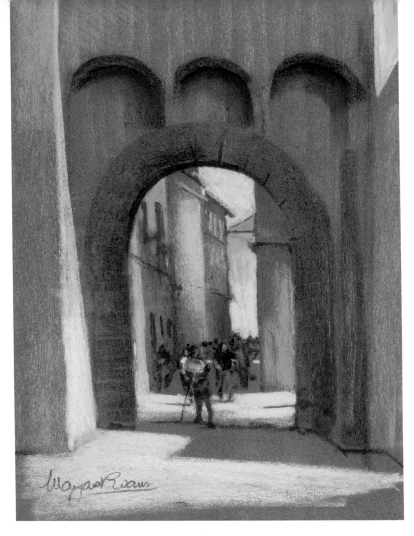

◀ **Pienza Gateway**
30 × 23 cm (12 × 9 in)
Looking through a
doorway or gate
helps to contain the
subject. Quickly
blocking in the
surround of this
frame allowed me to
spend more time on
the subject within.

QUICK OVERVIEW

☐ To begin a picture, take five minutes
to sketch in your composition, starting
with the large shapes.

☐ Block in the main areas of colour
then add intensity and tone by layering
on more pigment.

☐ In the final stages use blending to
smooth some areas in contrast to
textured ones.

☐ To practise getting down the
essentials, try 10-minute and five-
minute studies.

Simplifying shapes

Picture building is about seeing your subject in simple blocks and shapes that help the eye to move around the scene. With this ability to simplify, you will be confident to take on any subject no matter how complicated it first appears.

MATERIALS

Sennelier La Carte
  board in Sand
Thin dark green
  Conté stick
Soft pastels
Bright green
Creamy yellow
Golden brown
Golden orange
Greenish-ochre
Indigo
Light green
Pale blue
Pale cream
Purplish-grey
Red
Bluish green

1 Sketch in the outline shape of the buildings with the Conté stick, emphasizing the angle of the roofs and narrow street. Add strong light tones to the sky and pavement areas to give a sense of sunlight, using warm and cool colours respectively.

2 Put in the strongest shadows and link them together wherever possible to create a balanced composition of darks and lights. Using indigo, place the darkest tones under the roof eaves first, then add the slightly lighter shadows with purplish-grey.

3 Now that the main light and dark tones are positioned, block in the basic colours of the buildings, using greenish-ochre with pale cream on top. Lightly blend the colours over some of the shadows. Using indigo, roughly position the windows, doorways and figures.

◀ **Lucca Shoppers**
32 × 25 cm (12½ × 10 in)

4 Strengthen the building colours with a creamy yellow. Suggest a few details of the figures walking on the street – a dot of colour will be more effective than trying to draw in exact detail which would require pencils or thin sticks and take up too much time.

WORKING INDOORS

Working indoors tends to be more comfortable, so time does not seem so much of an issue. However, the discipline of keeping to a 30-minute time limit will act like a tonic to keep your work fresh and expressive – it is all too easy to work away at a painting until it is 'finished', not realizing that in fact it has been overworked.

Whether you are painting a still life, flowers or a portrait from life, or working from photographs, the discipline remains the same throughout – keep it simple. This approach encourages you to make sketches and preliminary works instead of facing the pressure of trying to create a finished painting every time.

◀ **Roses in Bloom**
20 × 25 cm (8 × 10 in)
I subdued the starkness of white paper by choosing some random pastel colours and washing them over the whole area. Once they were dry I painted the flowers on top.

Still life

The best way of motivating yourself to paint indoors is to set up a simple still life of a few personal possessions in the corner of a room and observe them from different angles. The great thing about 30-minute pastels is that you can fit your painting in between other jobs, and by leaving your still life subject out on show you can look at it every time you pass and consider how you will tackle it when you have the time.

Keep your choice of subject simple and be selective – too many objects will clutter and complicate the picture. Try a theme such as gardening items, children's toys or a particular colour scheme; random objects will not gel together and will make a less interesting impact.

Before launching into a composition of several objects together, it is a good idea to spend five minutes studying single, uncomplicated objects, such as a piece of fruit or a dish. This accustoms your eye to look not only for linear information but tonal values also.

◀ **Choosing a subject**
Choose simple, uncomplicated objects that can be grouped with others to make a theme.

▼ **Being selective**
Once you have set up an arrangement it is worth while making a quick sketch to simplify the shapes and check that the composition is well balanced.

▲ Still life group
This group is lit from one side to produce simple shadows. The high angle of view exaggerates the inside of the jug and enhances the ellipses and circles in the composition.

▶ Still Life
18 × 22 cm (7 × 8½ in)
The subject is placed on a green background to contrast with its warm oranges and browns and help to unify the picture. The shadows repeat the green background in dark green and highlights of palest green.

QUICK TIP

Restrict your still life to a limited number of objects and be selective about which part will be the focal point, giving it more detail than the other elements.

Flowers

A study of a single flower is ideal to start with for a 30-minute painting. This allows you to really observe the shape and structure of the flower and create the basic relationship between flower, stem and leaves. By sketching in each of these elements of the flower and then blocking in the main colours, you will have plenty of time left to work into the flower itself and create the texture and detail.

Grouping flowers

Within a bunch of flowers there should be two or three main 'character' flowers that will become the focal points. The remainder should be a supporting background, with much less detail, creating softer vignette backgrounds to the main flowers. If the paper is substantial enough to take water, washes over the background colours is an ideal technique for covering paper quickly and giving a fluid look to the painting.

◀ Rosebud
A rosebud can be blocked in with strong colour and darker tones added for shadows, creating a firm shape. A full-blown rose is more flimsy in outline.

▲ Foxglove
A foxglove is easily captured by drawing the stem in a single line and leaving some flowerheads without detail to create a softer, sketchy effect.

▶ Floral Group
In a floral group the light will fall on a particular bloom, which in turn will create shadows on the others.

Background influence

You can save time by selecting the background paper colour to complement the painting, making use of it in areas where the pastel is applied thinly. With a dark background the subject can be painted in to appear as if it is emerging from the shadows, which creates a dramatic effect in a short space of time. Similarly, a light paper can play a part in the composition for stronger-coloured flowers, especially when you are diluting pastels with water to create watercolour-style effects.

▶ **Hollyhocks**
45 × 30 cm (18 × 12 in)
The strong dark red paper gave me an excellent base for quickly blocking in the bright reds of the flowers and green areas for foliage. Gaps between the pastel applications show the paper colour, which enhances the subject.

◀ **Squared forms**
A box shape provides the basis for most types of building, both domestic and commercial.

◀ **Circles**
A circle gives a starting point for many animals. In larger animals there may be several.

◀ **Ovals**
Many subjects in nature, such as flowers, and in the home too are based on ovals.

Observing shapes

Your paintings will always benefit from any spare minutes you can spend at home observing ordinary everyday objects and considering their basic shapes. Whether you are planning a composition indoors or outdoors, this will help you to draw with speed and economy.

Finding geometric shapes

Most beginners dread tackling buildings, but seeing them as basic building blocks of squares or rectangles will make it easier to learn to draw them. At home, sketch some box shapes out of your head and turn them into building shapes, then look at some photographs of buildings and try to simplify them into boxes.

Similarly, you can turn circles into many subjects by embellishing the basic shape. Most flowers and many animals too can be started by drawing a series of circles or ovals.

Working up a composition

Take some everyday objects you see regularly and work out their basic shapes and how they interact when placed next to each other. Move the objects about and create different compositions, not only in portrait and landscape formats but also squares and panoramas – don't just limit yourself to the shape of the paper in front of you.

Use your imagination to create different compositions, making quick thumbnail sketches of those that look promising. Those sketches, even the ones you discard, will represent minutes well spent as you won't waste time drawing and painting a composition that is ultimately unsuccessful.

◄ **Choosing objects**
Everyday objects can provide an exercise in experimenting with composition. The shapes between them are just as important as they help tie everything together and balance the composition.

▲ **Trying different placings**
Before committing yourself to a painting, move the objects around and change the angle to create a different composition.

Portraits

To make a start with portraits it is helpful to observe people from a distance and practise doing quick sketches. These need not be full facial studies as side or rear views can equally capture the look of a person. With the same strategy you have used for other subjects, catching the large shapes of head and shoulders first before starting on facial features makes for speed and can also help you to achieve movement, especially if people are unaware of being watched.

Capturing the pose

Portraits can be recognizable even without features if the proportions of head to shoulders and a typical pose are captured and colour is simplified and bold. Someone who habitually sits in a slouched position, for example, will be easily distinguished from someone who sits upright, and standing figures in particular allow the artist to be expressive and exaggerate mannerisms that would otherwise not be noticed.

▲ **Indian Baby**
Outlining the shape of the baby in a white dress and blocking in the background colours made the shape stand out as light against dark, giving extra impact.

▶ **Portrait of John**
Catching people unawares is a great way to collect casual poses for adding into paintings later. By the time the person realizes you are sketching them the main work is done.

▲ **Indian Girl**
The pose is important to create the mood and character of the person. Our tour guide looked quite bored as she sat waiting for the group to arrive!

Simplifying features

If the features on portraits are too detailed the effect can be heavy, which can distort the likeness and sometimes add years to a person's face, particularly in the case of children's portraits. By softly simplifying and understating the details, an impression of the person is formed which leaves something to the imagination. This avoids the work being too photographic and saves valuable time, making a 30-minute pastel even easier to achieve.

▶ **Girl in Hat**
30 × 23 cm (12 × 9 in)
The dark blue paper shows off the strong light shape of the hat for impact and creates a cool balance against the warm pink and cream skin tones.

◀ **Portrait of Cody**
30 × 23 cm (12 × 9 in)
Using a light background allowed me to wet the first pastel applications to create a watercolour wash effect. Once they were dry, I built dry applications of pastel on top to create a soft blended effect for a child's skin.

Including props

Some people are particularly recognizable by the way they dress. Props such as hats and spectacles make the likeness easier to achieve as they act as distinguishing features. They are also helpful for taking measurements when you are placing the position of the features.

Hats and spectacles hide part of the face. Don't attempt to paint what you cannot see – stick to the features that are clearly visible.

Working from photographs

There is a great temptation to take a long time over a painting when you are working from a photograph. Comfortably settled at home, you will find it all too easy to settle into copying mode, where the drawing is meticulously reproduced and colour mixing becomes colour matching. Take a tip from the American watercolourist Ed Whitney, who once said, 'I don't want the truth, I want beautiful lies.' By selecting the important elements of a photograph and rejecting unimportant details, it is possible to give a fresh, personal rendition of the subject.

◀ **Tonal sketch**
When you are using a photograph it is helpful to spend a few minutes first on a quick tonal thumbnail sketch, working in pencil or hard pastel, and sketching main shapes to work out the composition.

◀ **Colour sketch**
Another way of quickly testing out a composition is to do a colour sketch without drawing, blocking in large areas of lights and darks without any details. Moving shapes around experimentally is always worth a try and gets you away from copying what is there already.

▲ **Market scene**
For a complicated scene, take lots of snaps to get the general shapes. You can then move these around in your composition as you wish. Incidental figures will come in useful for putting into many paintings.

Changing the format

A great way of exercising your imagination with a photograph is to take it in landscape format then see if it can successfully be changed to a portrait, square or panoramic format. Playing around with the composition rather than relying on the original format often produces great paintings.

When I am trying out different formats, I draw 'floating boxes' of varying shapes within the page of a sketchbook. This allows me to add or subtract to alter the outer shape, experiment with the format and recompose the picture. When the problems of composition have been worked out and improved I can then start on the final painting.

◀ **Square format**
A square format encloses the composition, which creates more focus on the people in the market and gives less importance on the buildings around.

◀ **Portrait format**
Another quick tonal sketch extends the buildings to include the sky and rooftops and gives a completely different mood to the scene.

▲ **Market scene**
This photograph was taken as a landscape format, but by trying out 'floating boxes'

within the page of a sketchbook I extended the sides to alter the composition and try more options.

QUICK TIP

Ask yourself 'Why did I take this photo? What was it that attracted me to the subject?' This helps you to see the point of the exercise rather than copying everything that is there.

◀ **Highland village**
Bland subjects in
photographs that
you don't have time
to paint on location
can be made more
exciting by switching
on the sunshine on
an otherwise dull
day and creating
new compositions in
pastel colours that
inspire you.

Capturing atmosphere

Adding atmosphere to an otherwise dull
photograph can improve the subject and
make it more imaginative. This is
particularly helpful where there is a lack
of detail available in a poor-quality
photograph, or where the weather
conditions have not been ideal for capturing
the image. The photograph becomes a
simple record of events and allows the
artist more scope to be expressive.

▶ **Highland Village**
24 × 35 cm (9½ × 14 in)
The two photographs
of this street were
both dull as it was
about to rain, but by
using elements of
each, recomposing
them into a new
landscape format
and adding sunshine
to give more depth
an interesting picture
was created.

◄ Market stalls 1
I liked the left side of the composition but felt that the right was rather nondescript and needed the introduction of another angle to bring the eye into the main market scene.

◄ Market stalls 2
The stall in in this photograph offered the ideal angle to add on to the composition and make a slightly panoramic format, which had the possibility of an interesting picture.

▲ Mirepoix Market
19 × 32 cm (7½ × 12½ in)
The light streams into the market square from the left and now gives a more enclosed feeling to the scene, with figures from both photographs used to add interest. The complicated subject at the back of the stalls is merely suggested to give a feeling of crowds.

Multiple photographs

Using several different photographs for reference, taking elements from each, can create new and exciting compositions. You will need to make sure that you keep the light coming in from a consistent source, and be particularly careful with proportion when you are placing subjects next to each other. Selecting the best points of each photograph also helps you to avoid the habit of copying what's actually there and be more creative.

QUICK OVERVIEW

☐ Keep still life groups simple and uncluttered when you are working within the 30-minute time frame.

☐ Look at every option possible to portray your subject – don't just accept the first angle you arrive at.

☐ Capture simplified large main shapes first before adding any detail.

☐ Use photographs creatively.

Painting a still life

By limiting this exercise to simply pastel pencils and hard pastels, it is easy to paint a still life quickly at home without making too much mess. It will also exercise both your drawing and painting skills in the space of 30 minutes.

MATERIALS

Canson Sand
  pastel paper
**Stabilo Carb
  Othello pencils**
Dark green
Dark grey
Ochre
White

Conté Carres sticks
Bright green
Bright red
Cadmium yellow
Orange
Pink
Warm grey

1 With your dark green pencil, sketch in the total outer shape of the flowers, hat and secateurs, ensuring that everything will fit on to the paper. No detail is needed as this simply sketches the plan and confirms the composition. Note the direction of the light source and add shading to establish tone.

2 Block in the colours using Conté sticks and pastel pencils, keeping the colour scheme simple and limited. Block in the tonal values to create the pattern of light on each object and leave the neutral paper for highlights. Note how the light background needs to be darkened slightly to allow the pale-coloured flowers to stand out.

3 Build up the final colours to create more details and texture. Continue to emphasize the light and shade by putting stronger contrasts against areas that need more impact - for example, adding white to the pale flowers against their darker background. Finally, blend some textured areas, such as part of the hat, to emphasize their rough texture elsewhere.

◀ **Still Life with Flowers**
28 × 38 cm (11 × 15 in)

WORKING OUTDOORS

Working outdoors is exciting, but it can be frustrating without a plan of action. That's why the 30-minute pastel is perfect for this situation. With some organizing, it is possible to set up simply, assess the subject quickly, take a photograph for reference later then go for it, keeping in mind the impact that is needed to convey to the viewer what attracted your attention in the first place.

I tell my students, 'Paint outdoors as if the bus is leaving without you in five minutes!' It's amazing what you can get down on paper in 10 minutes, or even five, and that leaves extra time for bonus work such as adding more detail in the landscape.

◀ **Cairns Beach, Australia**
24 × 33 cm (9½ × 13 in)
It was very hot yet windy weather when this was done – not a good day for working in pastels! A 20-minute impression of the long beaches gave enough detail, backed up with photographs for a later painting.

▶**Plockton,
Scotland**

33 × 50 cm (13 × 19½ in)
By wetting each
layer of pastel and
allowing the washes
to run together
and give a quick
impression, I
captured the bare
essentials in 10
minutes to create
the light of the
evening sun.

Simplifying
landscapes

The majority of landscapes can be divided
into distance, middle distance and
foreground; an open landscape may split
into sky, water and foreground. Putting
in the large shapes is the first step in
order to ensure that you are able to fit
everything you want on your paper. Learn
to see trees as a mass and rows of houses
as one shape. The mass shapes also help
to determine later where the quiet areas
of the painting can be, as opposed to the
busy parts, which will be screaming out
for attention to details.

Capturing the grand scale

A basic understanding of perspective will help you to dramatize the angles and viewpoints of a scene and capture the grand scale. Many panoramic or busy scenes seem too complicated and leave the artist not knowing where to begin, but remember that you do not have to copy exactly what you can see. By concentrating on those big shapes and making the eye level exciting, it is possible to create the feeling of grandeur.

◀ **Austrian Alps**
30 × 45 cm (12 × 18 in)
From the top of the ski lifts, the drama of looking down across the mountains is accentuated with a high eye level, creating plenty of room for showing the depths below and exaggerating the angles.

┃QUICK TIP

Painting contre-jour (against the light) helps you to see simplified outlines of shapes as the detail is bleached out by the light. This technique not only makes painting easier but looks more dramatic.

Painting trees

When you are tackling a single tree, imagine it is placed against the light and see just the profile. Make sure the span of its canopy fits into the space on the paper and measure how wide the tree is compared to its height. This helps to define whether the tree is tall and thin or short and wide. Keeping the background simple behind a feature tree will focus attention on the textural qualities of the tree and give it more impact.

◄ **Woodland Path**
20 × 28 cm (8 × 11 in)
Dark paper suggests the mystery of the woodland and blocks of thick pastel enhanced with some white gouache create a body of colour where the white cottage is. I added thicker highlights of pastel to the trees and diluted mid to darker tones with water to sink into the paper colour and create shadows.

▲ **Tree colours**
Never start by painting a brown trunk and green foliage as it makes the tree look like a child's painting. Generally trees are silhouetted against light sky, so a dark greenish-brown will capture the outer shape. Lighter greens and browns can be added later for detail if necessary.

Grouping trees

In a woodland scene, the main bulk of trees can be divided into distant, middle-ground and foreground trees. Portraying one or two main character trees in more detail will create focal points, but don't emphasize too many as this will make the painting 'bitty'. Use similar colours throughout to ensure unity and enhance the tonal differences.

Reflections in water

Observing how a single item such as a tree or building reflects in water will help you to understand the effect that water has on a mirror image. Ideally, find a quiet pond of calm water and look at the still reflection – squinting through half-closed eyes helps, as the mid-tones disappear and the subject is simplified into dark and light shapes.

Note how the still reflection lengthens the shape, and how it may be darker in tone than the shape itself. Now throw a stone into the water and observe how the ripples that are created distort the mirror shape and extend it into a wider, deeper shape, with wonderful jagged edges.

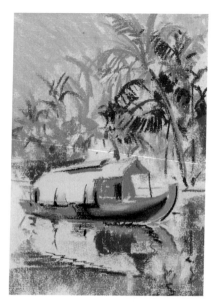

▲ **Rice Boat Reflections**
22 × 16 cm (8½ × 6½ in)
I built up the reflections at the same time as I painted each shape and colour on land, allowing the reflections to represent the water in its entirety.

▶ **Single Tree Reflections**
The colours of the single tree are repeated in the water area and blended with a downward stroke to create the impression of the depth of the water. Dragging a plastic eraser across reflections gives the appearance of surface movement.

Multiple reflections

Multiple shapes such as buildings create a pattern which lends itself almost to abstraction. To show distorted shapes in water, allow the vertical reflections to merge horizontally, making a fascinating pattern of colours. When you are painting reflections such as this it is easiest and quickest to block in the mirror image with vertical strokes to repeat the shapes above the water and give the appearance of its depth, then use a damp brush with horizontal strokes to create a zig-zag pattern, allowing the colours to knit together. Finally, adding some light reflections on the surface of the water will give further depth.

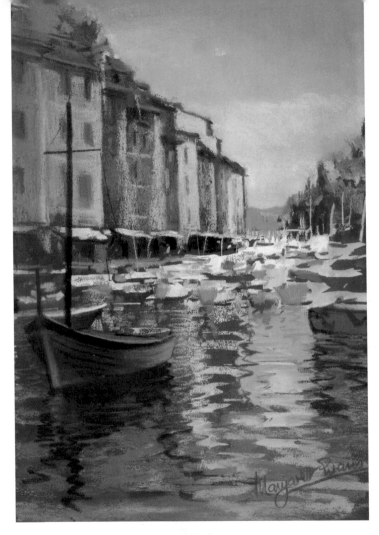

▶ **Portofino**
30 × 20 cm (12 × 8 in)
The emphasis on the stunning deep blue sea and sky helps to identify this scene instantly as a Mediterranean one. The blues create a strong cool balance against the warm terracotta colour of the buildings.

Skies

Even in the case of a clear blue sky, it is important to create a sense of perspective and depth by gradating the tone of blue. The sky at the top of the picture is closer, and is therefore usually stronger in colour; towards the horizon it becomes paler. Remembering this will help you to achieve quick and convincing results.

Painting clouds

All objects need highlights and shadows in order to appear three-dimensional, and exactly the same principle holds true when you are painting clouds. By using an off-white or creamy base colour to block in the cloud formations, you can then add the darker shadows beneath with a grey or purplish-blue and the highlights with white.

Dramatic sky effects

Although these basic formulas are very helpful to use for quick sky recipes, you must never forget to draw upon your own observation. It is not the case that clouds are invariably shadowed from beneath, nor is the lower part of the sky always lighter than the top. You will always see skies and cloud formations that break the rules, and this can add to the drama of a sky as it seizes the viewer's attention.

◀ **Clear skies**
A general formula for a clear blue sky is to make the blue stronger at the top of the painting, where the sky is nearer the viewer, and paler towards the horizon.

◀ **Clouds**
Negative painting around the cloud shapes with blue sky colour will position the clouds and give the basic shapes before darker colours are added to give the clouds more form and tone.

◀ **Dramatic skies**
Observation is the best way to learn how to capture dramatic skies, especially sunsets. This predominantly orange sky has palest turquoise and cream in the distance and dark clouds on the horizon.

▲ Evening Clouds
18 × 26 cm (7 × 10¼ in)
Because there are dark, dramatic clouds in the distance, the horizon is darker than the sky at the top of the picture. As here, evening clouds are often in the complementary colour of purple against the orange light from the sun.

▶ Looking up
If you are looking up at the subject, your eye level is low. There is not much foreground to fit in, as the majority of action will be above the eye level.

▶ On the level
A central eye level cuts the picture in half. Your painting will be improved by adjusting your eye level and putting more above or below the centre.

▶ Looking down
Looking down on a subject means that your eye level should be placed high on the paper, leaving plenty of room for the details below.

Buildings

With regard to perspective, when you are working quickly the most important point is to assess angles and, once you have recognized them, to exaggerate and dramatize them.

Work out your eye level first and draw a line across the paper to help remind you where it is. You can then see immediately whether the main content in the picture is above or below this line, and whether your eye level is low or high respectively. It is not good practice to place the eye level in the centre, so if you realize there is as much above the line as below, consider where there is more to emphasize then raise or drop that line slightly to avoid cutting the picture in half.

Vanishing points
Parallel lines leading towards the horizon converge at what is called the vanishing point, which will always be at eye level. In a 30-minute painting there is little time to spend on detailed perspective, but be aware of whether roof lines, for example, are going up or down to meet your eye level. Assessing roughly at which point a roof line would meet that eye level if it were extended will give you a vanishing point where all other parallel lines on the same house would meet.

Different moods

You can bring enormous variation to the same subject by exaggerating and altering angles and using different papers to change colours, backgrounds and textures. A very rough paper can create plenty of texture for old, crumbling buildings, and you can dramatize the mood and atmosphere by using a strong background paper colour.

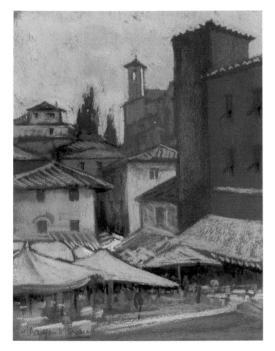

◀ **Montecatini 1**
32 × 25 cm (12½ × 10 in)
The evening glow of the Tuscan sun is enhanced with the warm tone of the red paper, which I left uncovered in places in order to add to the strength of the reds. I used a neutral blue grey to add coolness to the busy areas where people are milling around.

▶ **Montecatini 2**
32 × 25 cm (12½ × 10 in)
A cooler version of the same scene shows the different mood created by using a darker red paper, which still contributes warmth to the scene but is played against cooler stone colours on the buildings.

Figures

Adding human life to a scene will not only make it come alive but will add to the sense of scale, help to draw attention to a focal point, and make the whole scene more interesting.

Practising quick figures

Working on a general rule that the head is one eighth of the body, a stick can give a basic size for positioning a figure. Find the top eighth by halving it, then halving the top section twice more to give the proportion of the head.

From this point the shoulders are wide, then the body tapers down to below the halfway point. Beneath this you can position the legs to stand or walk. Practise plenty of varying positions and shapes to vary the characters.

Grouping figures

To show figure groups, block in blobs of colour then add heads and legs. This creates plenty of animation without the need for any details, which would take up valuable time.

◀ **Quick figures**
Most figures are seen as dark against light, so using a dark blue or brown simply sketch in a head, widen for the shoulders then taper down to the legs, always adding a shadow for volume.

◀ **Groups**
Having fun with bright splashes of colour, adding suggestions of heads and legs, will turn paint splodges into impressions of animated figures.

▼ Mexican Picnic
21 × 30 cm (8¼ × 12 in)
This sketch of a family having a picnic in the shade shows counterchanged figures against varying tones. The dark paper allows details like the legs and tree branches to blend into the shadows, and the sunny highlights give maximum contrast.

Counterchange

Positioning figures in the correct place is important for catching the eye or filling empty spaces, and tonal values play a large part in emphasizing them. Place a light figure against a dark background and vice versa to create more interest; this juxtaposition of dark and light is known as counterchange. Give less important figures less impact against their background.

◀ Counterchange
Putting some figures as light shapes against dark backgrounds, such as inside doorways, and balancing this with some dark figures against light adds tonal depth to paintings.

QUICK OVERVIEW

☐ Divide landscapes into distance, middle distance and foreground and look for mass shapes.

☐ Accentuate angles for drama.

☐ In a woodland scene, pick out one or two trees to create focal points.

☐ A clear blue sky is stronger in colour overhead than on the horizon; dark clouds may reverse this.

☐ Choose an eye line that is not exactly central in your picture.

☐ Add human figures to give scale and animation.

Painting a landscape

When you are working on location the light will change constantly, so it is important to get the large areas blocked in quickly to capture the moods and tonal contrasts before considering any details.

MATERIALS

Ingres off-white
  pastel paper
Light grey Conté
  Carres stick
Soft pastels
Blue grey
Bright green
Bright red

Burnt sienna
Cobalt blue
Dark brown
Indigo
Pale blue
Pale burnt sienna
Reddish brown

1 Begin by drawing the outline with the light grey pastel stick. Next block in the cool shadow colours with enough strength to ensure that they will still show through after you have subsequently blocked in the main colours.

2 As you build up the main colours the uniform texture of the paper will become apparent. Resist the temptation to start rubbing and smoothing this texture in places as it can be dealt with later – the changing colours and tones are first priority. Lay in basic colours first, exaggerating them slightly. Keep blended colours fresh and don't try to match nature.

3 Blend a few areas where the paper texture is still dominant and a smoother finish is needed. However, leave the combination of texture and colour mixes alone in the hillside to create the tapestry of colours in the landscape. Strengthen the tones, making darks darker and lights lighter, then add final touches of a few linear marks for detail to the house, bridge and castle.

◀ **Eilean Donan**
30 × 40 cm (12 × 18 in)

FURTHER INFORMATION

Here are some organizations or resources that you might find useful to help you to develop your painting.

Art Magazines
The Artist, Caxton House, 63/65 High Street, Tenterden, Kent TN30 6BD; tel: 01580 763673
www.painters-online.co.uk
Artists & Illustrators, 26-30 Old Church Street, London SW3 5BY; tel: 020 7349 3150
www.aimag.co.uk
International Artist, P. O. Box 4316, Braintree, Essex CM7 4QZ; tel: 01371 811345
www.artinthemaking.com
Leisure Painter, Caxton House, 63/65 High Street, Tenterden, Kent TN30 6BD; tel: 01580 763315
www.painters-online.co.uk

Art Materials
Daler-Rowney Ltd, P. O. Box 10, Bracknell, Berkshire RG12 8ST; tel: 01344 461000
www.daler-rowney.com
Jackson's Art Supplies Ltd, 1 Farleigh Place, London N16 7SX; tel: 0870 241 1849
www.jacksonsart.co.uk

T. N. Lawrence & Son Ltd, 208 Portland Road, Hove, West Sussex BN3 5QT; tel: 0845 644 3232 or 01273 260260
www.lawrence.co.uk
Winsor & Newton, Whitefriars Avenue, Wealdstone, Harrow, Middlesex HA3 5RH; tel: 020 8427 4343
www.winsornewton.com

Art Shows
Affordable Art Fair, The Affordable Art Fair Ltd, Unit 3 Heathmans Road, London SW6 4TJ; tel: 020 7371 8787
www.affordableartfair.co.uk
Art in Action, Waterperry House, Waterperry, Nr Wheatley, Oxfordshire OX33 1JZ; tel: 020 7381 3192 (for information)
www.artinaction.org.uk
Patchings Art, Craft & Design Festival, Patchings Art Centre, Patchings Farm, Oxton Road, Calverton, Nottinghamshire NG14 6NU; tel: 0115 965 3479
www.patchingsartcentre.co.uk

Art Societies
The Pastel Society, 17 Carlton House Terrace, London SW1Y 5BD; tel: 020 7930 6844
www.thepastelsociety.org.uk
Society for All Artists (SAA), P. O. Box 50, Newark, Nottinghamshire NG23 5GY; tel: 01949 844050
www.saa.co.uk

Bookclubs for Artists
Artists' Choice, P. O. Box 3, Huntingdon, Cambridgeshire PE28 0QX; tel: 01832 710201
www.artists-choice.co.uk
Painting for Pleasure, Brunel House, Newton Abbot, Devon TQ12 4BR; tel: 0870 44221223
www.readersunion.co.uk

Internet Resources
Art Museum Network: the official website of the world's leading art museums
www.amn.org
Artcourses: an easy way to find part-time classes, workshops and painting holidays in Britain and Europe
www.artcourses.co.uk

The Arts Guild: on-line bookclub
www.artsguild.co.uk
British Arts: useful resource for all
art-related matters
www.britisharts.co.uk
British Library Net: comprehensive A-Z
resource including 24-hour virtual
museum/gallery
www.britishlibrary.net/museums.html
Galleries: the UK's largest-circulating
monthly art listings magazine
www.artefact.co.uk
Galleryonthenet: provides member artists
with gallery space on the internet
www.galleryonthenet.org.uk
Margaret Evans: the author's website, with
details of her workshops, holidays, books,
DVDs, and a gallery of her paintings
www.shinafoot.co.uk
Open College of the Arts: an open-access
college, offering home-study courses to
students worldwide
www.oca-uk.com
Painters Online: practical art site run by
The Artist's Publishing Company and
packed with information and inspiration
for all artists
www.painters-online.co.uk

WWW Virtual Library: extensive
information on galleries worldwide
www.comlab.ox.ac.uk/archive/other/
museums/galleries.html

Videos

APV Films, 6 Alexandra Square,
Chipping Norton, Oxfordshire OX7 5HL;
tel: 01608 641798
www.apvfilms.com
Teaching Art, P. O. Box 50, Newark,
Nottinghamshire NG23 5GY;
tel: 01949 844050
www.teachingart.com

FURTHER READING
Why not have a look at other art
instruction titles from Collins?

Balkwill, Ray, *Learn to Paint Coastal
    Landscapes*
Bellamy, David, *Learn to Paint Watercolour
    Landscapes*
Blockley, Ann, *Watercolour Textures*
Crawshaw, Alwyn, *Alwyn Crawshaw's
    Ultimate Painting Course*
  30-minute Sketching
French, Soraya, *30-minute Acrylics*

Jennings, Simon, *Collins Artist's Colour
    Manual*
  Collins Complete Artist's Manual
Keal, Jenny, *Learn to Paint Landscapes in
    Pastel*
King, Ian, *Gem Watercolour Tips*
Peart, Fiona, *30-minute Watercolours*
Simmonds, Jackie, *Gem Sketching*
Simmonds, Jackie, Wendy Jelbert and
    Marie Blake, *Need to Know? Drawing
    & Sketching*
Soan, Hazel, *Gem 10-minute Watercolours*
  *Learn to Paint Light and Shade in
    Watercolour*
  Secrets of Watercolour Success
Trevena, Shirley, *Vibrant Watercolours*
Waugh, Trevor, *Winning with Watercolour*
Whitton, Judi, *Loosen up your Watercolours*

For further information about Collins
books visit our website:
www.collins.co.uk

INDEX